AF481267

Alfie at Soca Farm

Alfie at Soca Farm was created to help kids learn the sounds of different animals,
as well as the days of the week, using the genre of soca music.

"Soca" refers to a genre of music that is derived from "soul calypso," or calypso music.
It creates a lively and energetic sound with infectious rhythms, driven by instruments,
such as drums and steel pans that are a central element that gets people moving.
The lyrics of soca songs often focus on joy, celebration, and a festive atmosphere.
Soca music is particularly popular in the Caribbean.
It has also gained international recognition and is enjoyed by audiences around the world.

Learning animal sounds enhances language skills in preschoolers
by introducing them to new vocabulary.
They associate specific sounds with corresponding animals.
This contributes to language acquisition and pronunciation.
Recognizing and imitating animal sounds encourages memory recall which is crucial
for the overall development of a child's brain.
This multi-sensory experience also enhances their overall perception and
understanding of the world around them.

Enjoy learning with Alfie!

Alfie

loves

____

Name

SOCA FARM

Welcome
to
Soca Farm!

SOCA FARM

Rooster says
Cock-a-doodle-doo.
He wakes up the
Sunday Crew.

SOCA FARM

Cow says
moo moo moo.

Hen says
cluck cluck cluck.

Duck says
quack quack quack.

They dance and play
and eat all day.

Then they go
fast asleep.

SOCA FARM

Rooster says
Cock-a-doodle-doo.
He wakes up the
Monday Crew

SOCA FARM

Pig says
oink oink oink.

Goose says
honk honk honk.

Sheep says
baa baa baa.

They dance and play
and eat all day.

GOOD NIGHT

Then they go
fast asleep.

SOCA FARM

Rooster says
Cock-a-doodle-doo
He wakes up the
Tuesday Crew.

SOCA FARM

Dog says
woof woof woof.

Cat says
meow meow meow.

Bird says
tweet tweet tweet.

They dance and play
and eat all day.

Then they go
fast asleep.

SOCA FARM

Rooster says
Cock-a-doodle-doo.
He wakes up the
Wednesday Crew.

SOCA FARM

Mule says
heehaw heehaw heehaw.

Horse says
neigh neigh neigh.

Turkey says
gobble gobble gobble.

They dance and play
and eat all day.

RELAX

Then they go
fast asleep.

SOCA FARM

Rooster says
Cock-a-doodle-doo.
He wakes up the
Thursday Crew.

SOCA FARM

Dove says
coo coo coo.

Bee says
buzz buzz buzz.

Bull says
snort snort snort.

They dance and play
and eat all day.

Then they go
fast asleep.

SOCA FARM

Rooster says
Cock-a-doodle-doo.
He wakes up the
Friday Crew.

SOCA FARM

Goat says
baa baa baa.

Rabbit says
squeak squeak squeak.

Snake says
hiss hiss hiss.

They dance and play
and eat all day.

Then they go
fast asleep.

SOCA FARM

Rooster says
Cock-a-doodle-doo.
He wakes up the
Saturday Crew.

SOCA FARM

Squirrel says
squeak squeak squeak.

Frog says
ribbit ribbit ribbit.

Cricket says
chirp chirp chirp.

They dance and play
and eat all day.

Then they go
fast asleep.

SOCA FARM

All is quiet at Soca Farm. The week has come to an end.

SOCA FARM

Rooster says
Cock-a-doodle-doo
and the week
starts again.

The End.